THE ELECTORAL COLLEGE is under attack because it matters. Presidential elections determine who will direct federal agencies and appoint judges, but presidential campaigns also shape American politics. The Electoral College forces parties to build broad coalitions. It protects the power of states to run their own elections. And it contains disputes within individual states and reduces the risks from fraud.

Get rid of the Electoral College, and big cities will gain power at the expense of rural areas and small states. Political party coalitions will break down, encouraging fringe parties and spoiler candidates. In a more crowded field, a candidate could win with a small plurality. Differences among state election laws and an increased risk of fraud will compel a federal takeover of elections.

Of course, some politicians see these as features rather than bugs. Rep. Alexandria Ocasio-Cortez mocked rural America in a video against the Electoral College. Sen. Elizabeth Warren said the Electoral College

[

stands in the way of "national voting." Hundreds of proposed constitutional amendments to get rid of the Electoral College have failed in Congress, but now a campaign to hijack the Electoral College in favor of a national popular vote has gathered momentum.

All this would surprise the founders. Both the Federalist architects of the Constitution and their Anti-Federalist opponents found the Electoral College a reasonable way to select the president. In the ratification debates, the Anti-Federalists barely mentioned it at all. Alexander Hamilton, writing in *The Federalist Papers*, said of the Electoral College, "If it be not perfect, it is at least excellent."

What happened? And how much does it matter? Electoral College opponents simply

---

Alexander Hamilton said of the Electoral College, "If it be not perfect, it is at least excellent."

---

want to elect the president the same way we choose other elected officials. One person, one vote, right? Every state governor is chosen by a statewide popular vote. So why not a national popular vote for president?

THE ELECTORAL COLLEGE AND THE CONSTITUTION

The framers of the Constitution considered a popular vote and a parliamentary system. They rejected both and created the Electoral College. After months of intermittent debate, they were satisfied with their creation but unsure how it would work. In practice, it did work differently than many of them had expected. Rather than a body of wise men who proposed candidates for president who were then chosen by the House of Representatives, the founders themselves quickly turned the Electoral College into a two-step, democratic process.

In fact, the Electoral College almost certainly works better than the founders expected. After the minor (but important) changes made by the Twelfth Amendment in 1804, the constitutional structure of the Electoral College has remained the same for more than two centuries.

Why the Founders Created the Electoral College

Before the Constitution, the Articles of Confederation had established just a simple unicameral legislature. All the national legislative, executive, and judicial powers, such as they were, were in the hands of Congress. It was government by committee, and it was a mess. There was broad agreement that any remodel or replacement of the Articles would include an executive branch of government. What that might look like, however, was an open question.

Indeed, there was a moment of awkward silence at the Constitutional Convention when the topic first came up. Delegates had started work on Monday, May 28, and the Virginia Plan was introduced the next day. It was the first draft of what would become the new Constitution, and it called for "a National Executive ... to be chosen by the National Legislature." The delegates debated federal powers on Wednesday and the composition of Congress on Thursday, then turned to the executive on Friday.

Right away, according to James Madison's notes, Pennsylvania's James Wilson "moved that the Executive consist of a single person." When this motion received a second, there was a "considerable pause" until the chairman asked if the delegates were prepared to vote. Ben Franklin intervened, insisting "that the gentlemen would deliver their sentiments" on such "a point of great importance." In the ensuing debate, a unitary executive was declared alternately "the fetus of monarchy" and "the best safeguard against tyranny." The delegates postponed the question and moved on.

Later that same day, the Convention considered how to select the executive (or executives). Wilson spoke up again and said that he was "in theory" for a popular election. He wanted executive and legislative officials all elected by the people "in order to make them as independent as possible of each other." Roger Sherman from Connecticut supported the Virginia Plan's parliamentary system, arguing that the executive should be "absolutely dependent" on the legislature. Virginia's George Mason thought a popular election "impracticable" but hoped Wilson would "have time to digest it into his own form." Another delegate suggested election by the Senate alone, and then the Convention adjourned for the evening.

When they reconvened Saturday morning, Wilson had taken Mason's advice. He presented a plan to create districts and hold popular elections to choose electors. These electors would then vote for the national executive. In other words, Wilson proposed an electoral college. But with many details left out, and uncertainty about the nature of the executive office, Wilson's proposal was voted down eight to two (Pennsylvania and Maryland voted in favor).

The next Monday, the Convention agreed on a unitary executive – just one person would be president of the United States. The rest of the week was spent on other business, until Saturday. That morning Massachusetts delegate Elbridge Gerry proposed that state governors elect the president. This was voted down, but a theme appeared. Most delegates did not defend the Virginia Plan's parliamentary model; they simply found related flaws with the alternatives. The selection process needed to produce a president of character and ability without making him beholden to other politicians.

Members of Congress would know a lot about potential presidents. That insider knowledge could be useful in choosing someone of good character and ability to run the executive branch. But giving Congress power to select presidents – along with power to remove them through impeachment – would make the executive branch subservient to the legislative branch. At best, the president would not be independent; at worst, the office would be awarded based on corrupt backroom deals. And if any other group of politicians chose the president, the potential for control and corruption was the same.

One idea was that Congress could appoint the executive, but only electors chosen by states could renew the appointment. But the most bizarre proposal came from James Wilson, who suggested that members of Congress draw lots – actually, different colored balls out of a jar. The ones with the golden balls would be locked in a room until they chose a new president. In what may be the only joke recorded at the Constitutional Convention, Virginia's George Mason remarked two days later that "a lottery has been introduced. But as the tickets do not appear to be in much demand ... nothing therefore need be said on that subject."

The possibility of a direct election by the people came up again and again. It would keep the president independent and reduce the risk of corruption. On the other hand, how would the people know who was really fit to lead? This was not an aristocratic insult to the voters but a practical reality. In the 1790 census, the United States had fewer than 4 million people. Divide them into states and congressional districts, and many voters would have firsthand knowledge of their candidates for the House and Senate. Combine all the country's voters, and the percentage with personal

---

The selection process would need to produce a president of character and ability without making him beholden to other politicians.

---

knowledge of presidential candidates would be very small.

One argument not made for direct election was that it was democratic. The framers had already created the "democratic branch" of government: the House of Representatives. It operated according to the "democratic principle," as James Madison explained, as a "security for the rights of the people." No bill could become law without passing the House, and it had exclusive power to initiate taxes. The president did not need to represent the people but to put into effect the decisions of the people's representatives in Congress.

After two months, the Convention was still going in circles on how to select the president. On July 25, Madison argued that "The Option before us [is] between an appointment by Electors chosen by the people – and an immediate appointment by the people." Madison said he preferred election by the people, but he recognized two legitimate concerns. First, voters likely would prefer candidates from their own state, giving an advantage to larger states. Second, areas with higher concentrations of voters would have more power.

Madison identified this second concern with the southern states. This has given rise to claims that his eventual support for the Electoral College was simply a ploy to bolster the power of slave states. Yet Virginia was the largest state by population whether you include enslaved people or not. Pennsylvania, with almost no slaves, had the second-largest population, even counting slaves in other states. Southern states did have, on average, smaller populations – much smaller if you exclude slaves. But the most important rebuttal is what happened next.

Wrapping up his speech, Madison dismissed his own argument. Southern populations would grow, he said, and "local considerations must give way to the general interest." It was Oliver Ellsworth from Connecticut – a New England state – who then jumped in to defend small states and argue against a direct election. Ellsworth had earlier introduced the Connecticut Compromise that broke the deadlock between large and small states over Congress: representation in the House would depend on population, but states would have equal representation in the Senate.

Claims that "small state" arguments were about defending slavery are contradicted by the fact that there were plenty of small states in the north. Ellsworth's Connecticut was actually about average – Maine, New Hampshire, Rhode Island, and Vermont had much smaller populations. Also worth remembering is that slavery was legal in most of the north and had plenty of opponents in the south.

While Madison had argued half-heartedly for a direct election, he also had spoken positively about an electoral college, finding "very little opportunity for cabal, or corruption" in such a system. Other delegates repeated concerns about small states being ignored in a direct election and raised additional objections. Gerry, from Massachusetts, said a "popular election [would be] radically vicious" because it would, in effect, hand over power to organizations capable of manipulating public opinion. Another delegate worried that a national election would become "complex and unwieldy."

By August 31, the new Constitution was nearly finished – except for the process of electing the president. The question was put in the hands of a committee made up of one delegate from each of the eleven states represented at the Convention. That committee, which included Madison, presented its plan on September 4, and it was adopted the next day with minor changes.

What the Constitution Says

The Electoral College is described in Article II, Section 1, of the Constitution. It says:

> *Each State shall appoint, in such Manner as the Legislature thereof may direct, a Number of Electors, equal to the whole Number of Senators and Representatives to which the State may be entitled in the Congress.*

Each state gets at least three electors – two for its senators and one for each of its representatives in the House. This borrows directly from the Connecticut Compromise. Small states get a boost based on their two senators, but larger states get more electors based on their representatives. State legislatures decide how to select their state's electors. The paragraph concludes with a prohibition against federal officials serving as electors (Oregon Republicans had one elector disqualified in 1876 because he was a deputy postmaster).

The next paragraph explains how electors would vote.

> *The Electors shall meet in their respective States, and vote by Ballot for two Persons, of whom one at least shall not be an Inhabitant of the same State with themselves.... The Person having the greatest Number of Votes shall be the President, if such Number be a Majority.... In every Case, after the Choice of the President, the Person having the greatest Number of Votes of the Electors shall be the Vice President.*

It takes a majority of electoral votes to become president. If no candidate has a majority, or if there is a tie, then the House of Representatives elects the president. In this "contingency election," each state's delegation casts one vote, and a majority vote of all states is required to win.

The Twelfth Amendment Tweak

The original presidential election process, used in the first four elections, made the runner-up vice president. If there was a tie, the choice fell to the Senate. The first two elections were easy – almost everyone wanted George Washington as president, and John Adams provided geographic balance as vice president. Alexander Hamilton worked behind the scenes to ensure that there were fewer electoral votes for Adams than for Washington, so the right man ended up in the expected office.

The framers had already created the "democratic branch" of government: the House of Representatives.

Things were not so easy in 1796 when Washington declined to serve a third term. Adams, the leading man of the Federalist Party, just barely won the election. His nemesis, Thomas Jefferson of the Democratic-Republican Party, came in second. This led to a tumultuous administration rife with infighting and intrigue. And the election of 1800 was worse. Jefferson's unscrupulous running mate, Aaron Burr, tried to parlay an accidental deadlock into his own election by the House. Hamilton finally persuaded some Federalists in the House to vote for Jefferson, but the runner-up provision had proven too dangerous to remain in the Constitution.

The Twelfth Amendment, ratified in 1804, changed the Constitution so that electors "vote by ballot for President and Vice-President." Because the vice-presidential election is separate, it also requires a majority of electoral votes, or else the choice goes to the Senate.

Constitutional changes since the Twelfth Amendment have been minor: protecting voting rights in state elections to select presidential electors and granting three electors to the District of Columbia. Otherwise, the structure of the Electoral College has remained the same for over two centuries.

THE ELECTORAL COLLEGE IN PRACTICE

It is one thing to write the rules and something else to play the game. The founders became the first generation of politicians. As soon as the Constitution was in place, they set to work within the structures they had created. In the case of the Electoral College, this produced some surprises. It also established the practices that continue today.

In Such Manner as the Legislature Thereof May Direct

While the Constitution sets the framework, state legislatures decide how to choose their state's presidential electors. Legislatures have used their power in various ways. Some, especially in the first few elections, directly appointed electors. Others divvied up their electors, allowing voters to cast ballots for individual elector candidates or electing them from districts (or using existing congressional districts). After 1796, Jefferson's supporters realized they might have won if only Virginia had awarded all its electors based on the statewide popular vote. This winner-take-all system maximizes the power of a state within the Electoral College, and it became the way most states choose their electors.

Today, forty-eight states and the District of Columbia select their electors based on the statewide (or districtwide) popular vote. In Maine and Nebraska, voters in each congressional district choose one elector, and the remaining two are chosen based on the statewide vote. (In 2016, Donald Trump won a single elector in Maine; in 2008, Barack Obama won a single elector in Nebraska.) Both methods are legitimate ways of using the Electoral College.

Faithless?

One early change upended an assumption made by the founders, even though it had nothing to do with federal or state laws. They had expected that electors would exercise their own judgment, which made sense in a world without political parties. This arguably happened in the first two elections; then again, the outcome was a foregone conclusion. The rise of national parties, the Twelfth Amendment, and simple human nature created a new expectation: that electors would commit to vote for a particular candidate.

Ironically, the Constitution itself launched the two-party system. Ratification of the Constitution required a national debate – it cut across regional divides and featured only two sides. The sides in that debate evolved into the two parties. The founders had warned against political parties; then they became the first partisans.

If a party wants to win an office, the first step is to select just one of its members to compete. Otherwise it will spread its votes among multiple candidates and dilute its voting power. In other words, it was natural for the Federalists and Democratic-Republicans to nominate one candidate and then expect its other members – including those selected as electors – to support that candidate. This was only more true after the Twelfth Amendment, when electors could cast just one vote for president and a separate vote for vice president.

Eventually, the assumption that electors would vote for their party's nominee led to the epithet "faithless elector" to describe those who vote for someone else. Some states have passed laws to punish or prohibit electors from exercising their own judgement. It is easy to forget that electors are real people serving in a constitutional office with the duty of casting electoral votes for president and vice president. State laws to control how they cast their votes are likely unconstitutional, and as this book goes to print, the Supreme

Court is set to take up challenges to such laws from Colorado and Washington state.

However the court decides, the disputes are a tempest in a teacup. In the modern era, state political parties nominate their own members to serve as presidential electors. The party that wins in a state (or congressional district in Maine or Nebraska) has its nominees become the state's electors. They are partisans, well vetted by their own party, and often bound by an oath to their party to support its nominee. When electors do go rogue, they are usually on the losing side and simply trying to wage some sort of protest rather than throw an election.

The Electoral College borrows directly from the Connecticut Compromise.

Why the Electoral College Matters

It is easy to forget that when we vote for president, we really vote for electors who have pledged to support the candidate we favor. Civics education is not what it used to be, and perhaps the Electoral College is also a victim of its own success. Most of the time, it shapes American politics in ways that are beneficial but hard to see. When its effects do jump into the open, that is because some candidate and political party has just lost a hard-fought and narrowly decided election.

What are these beneficial effects? To put it another way, if James Madison were here with us today, what would he want to know about these last two centuries in order to judge the success of the Electoral College, and what conclusions would he reach?

Containing Disputes and Clarifying Results

One obvious result of the Electoral College is a practical respect for states, both their boundaries and their legislatures, in the presidential election process. While the federal government has assumed many powers once left to the states, running elections remains primarily a state function. The current system contains presidential elections within state lines, allowing elections to remain relatively decentralized. Of course, some see this as a flaw. Sen. Elizabeth Warren has explicitly linked her support for abolishing the Electoral College with her desire to increase federal power over elections. At a CNN town hall in March, Warren called for a constitutional amendment to replace the Electoral College with "national voting."

Containing elections within states, however, brings another benefit. The Electoral College uses state boundaries like the watertight bulkheads on an ocean liner. Disputes over mistakes or fraud are contained within individual states rather than spilling over into a need for nationwide recounts or greater federal control.

This was important in America's messiest

presidential election – which was not in 2000 but in 1876. That was the first time a candidate won an electoral vote majority while another candidate received more popular votes. (Some say it was 1824, but it was the House that elected John Quincy Adams over Andrew Jackson, and legislatures in six states had directly appointed electors.) The 1870s saw the rise of organized, systemic voter suppression in the south. Tiny margins and obvious fraud led to fierce disputes over vote totals in Florida, Louisiana, and South Carolina. Each of those states sent to Congress two sets of electoral vote totals – one favoring Republican Rutherford Hayes and the other favoring Democrat Samuel Tilden.

Just two days before inauguration day, Congress finished counting the votes – which included determining which votes to count – and declared Hayes the winner. Democrats proclaimed this "the fraud of the century." There is simply no way to tell, looking back, which side should have won. There was probably no way to tell at the time. It is clear that racist voter suppression would become an important part of the Democrats' hold on political power in the contested states. At the

---

Winner-take-all maximizes the power of a state within the Electoral College.

---

very least, the Electoral College contained these disputes within individual states so that Congress could endeavor to sort it all out. It is entirely possible that the Electoral College prevented voter fraud from stealing the White House.

The next election, in 1880, shows another effect of the constitutional system: it often amplifies the result. The popular vote margin that year was less than ten thousand votes, or just about .1 percent. Neither candidate had a popular vote majority, which is often the case in close presidential elections. Yet James Garfield won a resounding victory, with 214 electoral votes to Winfield Hancock's 155. There was no question who won, let alone any need for a recount. The Electoral College often bolsters the legitimacy of plurality winners. This was true in 1992, when Bill Clinton received just 43 percent of the popular vote but over 68 percent of the electoral votes.

Balance and Moderation

Perhaps the greatest benefit of our state-by-state election process is the powerful incentive it creates against regionalism. This is always true but easiest to see in the late nineteenth century. In 1888, incumbent President Grover Cleveland lost reelection despite receiving a popular vote plurality. This happened because he won big in the south. Cleveland's national popular vote margin was 94,530, but he won Texas by 146,461 votes. Altogether he won six states with margins greater than 30 percent, while only tiny Vermont delivered with such zeal for Republican Benjamin Harrison.

The election showed that, because of the

Electoral College, radical support in one region of the country was not going to be enough to win the White House. But Democrats already knew this. After the Civil War, and especially after the end of Reconstruction, the strength of the party was in the south. Yet Democrats nominated no southerners for either president or vice president between 1872 and 1928 (excluding West Virginia, which had remained with the north during the war). Both Cleveland and his running mate were northerners, and just like Al Gore in 2000, if Cleveland had only won his own home state, he would have become president.

Winning the presidency requires something more than a raw popular vote majority; it requires winning enough states to earn a majority in the Electoral College. Cleveland came back in 1892 to do just that. He actually received a smaller plurality of the popular vote (the Populist Party that year got 8.5 percent), but Cleveland won his home state of New York and his running mate's home state of Illinois, and he also picked up Indiana, Wisconsin, and California. This geographically broader coalition gave him a resounding Electoral College majority.

And so it goes. Whether we see it or not, the Electoral College pushes parties and their presidential campaigns to build broad coalitions and then to focus on the most closely divided states. This has become a popular attack on the system – swing states get a lot of attention, and other voters feel left out. Yet more Americans today live in highly partisan congressional districts than in "safe states." And the very legitimacy of a political party rests on all those safe states – on places that the party has already won over, thus allowing it to reach farther out. In 2000, George W. Bush needed every state that he won – not just Florida – to become president.

Every state matters, and every vote within a state matters – at least as much as in elections for governor or senator that may sometimes be very close and other times hopelessly one-sided. The Electoral College does put a premium on states that happen to be the most balanced in a particular election. Would we really prefer it if the path to the presidency was driving up the vote total in the deepest red or deepest blue states?

Consider one more quality of swing states: they are those most likely to have divided government. And if divided government is good for anything, it's accountability. In other words, the way the Electoral College works out, when we do wind up with a razor-thin margin, at least it is likely to happen in a state where both parties have some power rather than in a state where one party controls everything.

Desperately Seeking Democracy

Despite the benefits of the Electoral College, detractors maintain that it is unseemly for a candidate to win without receiving the most popular votes. Then-First Lady Hillary Clinton said in 2000 that "in a democracy, we should respect the will of the people and to me, that means it's time to do away with the Electoral College." Yet similar systems prevail around the world. In parliamentary systems – including in Canada, Israel, and the United Kingdom, to name a few – prime ministers are elected by the legislature. Germany and India do this but also have presidents who are elected by a combination of legislative bodies that form, dare I say it, an electoral college. In all these democratic systems, the national popular vote total is irrelevant.

And right here at home, what matters most about every legislative body, from the Oklahoma House of Representatives to the United States Senate, is which party is in control.

The founders had warned against political parties; then they became the first partisans.

That party elects leadership and sets the agenda. And in neither chamber of Congress nor in any of the ninety-nine state legislative chambers does the aggregate popular vote determine who is in charge. What matters is winning districts or states.

Nevertheless, there is a clamor of voices calling for an end to the Electoral College. Some is just sour grapes and posturing. Decrying this part of the Constitution has become an emblem of the "resistance," and it fits neatly within the progressive idea that whatever might help them obtain power must be progress. Hillary Clinton said in 2019 that we have "evolved" beyond the Electoral College. Former Attorney General Eric Holder has declared it "a vestige of the past," and Washington Governor Jay Inslee identified it as one of several "archaic relics of a bygone age." Indeed, prominent Democrats from Beto O'Rourke to Elizabeth Warren have jumped at opportunities to call for abolishing the Electoral College.

In fact, what some of these Democrats or their advisors might realize is just how similar their party's position is today to what it was in the late nineteenth century. California is becoming for them what the south was for their forerunners. The Golden State accounted for 10.4 percent of votes cast in 2016, while the southern states (from South Carolina to Florida and across to Texas) accounted for 10.6 percent of the votes cast in 1888. Cleveland won those southern states by nearly 39 percent, and Clinton won California by 30 percent. In other words, rather than building the broader coalition required to win the Electoral College, they would change the rules to increase the chances that their current, narrower coalition can win.

Whether for posturing or politics, calls to amend the Constitution are a dime a dozen. Even anti–Electoral College amendments with bipartisan support in the 1950s and 1970s failed to receive the required two-thirds supermajorities in order to be sent to the states for consideration. Partisan amendments will not make it through Congress, nor could they win ratification among the states.

The Dangerous Campaign for a National Popular Vote

There is a serious threat to the Electoral College, however. Until recently, it has gone mostly unnoticed as it has made its way through various state legislatures. If it works according to its supporters' intent, it will nullify the Electoral College and wipe away its benefits by creating a de facto direct election for president. How is this possible without constitutional change?

The National Popular Vote Interstate Compact, or NPV, takes advantage of the flexibility granted to state legislatures in the Constitution: "Each State shall appoint, in such Manner as the Legislature thereof may direct, a Number of Electors." The original intent is to allow legislators to determine how best to represent their states in presidential elections. The electors represent the state – not just the legislature – even though the latter has the power to direct the manner of appointment. But NPV supporters argue that this power allows legislatures to ignore their own state's voters and instead appoint electors based on the popular vote nationwide. This is what the compact would require states to do.

Of course, no state would do this unilaterally, so NPV has a trigger: it only takes effect if adopted by enough states that they control 270 electoral votes – in other words, a majority that would control the outcome of presidential elections. So far, fifteen states and the District of Columbia have signed on, with a total of 196 electoral votes.

Until 2019, every state that had joined NPV was deep-blue: California, Connecticut, Hawaii, Illinois, Maryland, Massachusetts, New Jersey, New York, Rhode Island, Vermont, and Washington. The NPV campaign has struggled to win more moderate blue states – Delaware and Oregon only adopted it in 2019. Following the 2018 election, Democrats' new "trifectas" (control of both legislative chambers and the executive) in purple Colorado and New Mexico wasted no time joining NPV. Others have not – Democratic legislators have so far blocked the measure in Maine, New Hampshire, and Virginia, and the governor of Nevada, also a Democrat, vetoed an NPV bill in 2019.

If NPV ever takes effect, it will have all the same effects as abolishing the Electoral College outright. Fraud in one state would affect every state, and the only way to deal with it would be to give more power to the federal government. An especially close election would require a nationwide recount. Candidates could win based on intense support from a narrow region or small collection of big cities.

NPV's jury-rigged direct election system would bring some unique risks as well. Despite its name, the plan cannot actually create a national popular vote. Each state would still – for the time being – run its own elections. This means a patchwork of rules for everything from which candidates are on the ballot

The Electoral College uses state boundaries like the watertight bulkheads on an ocean liner.

to how disputes are sorted out. It would reward states with lax election laws – the higher the turnout, legal or not, the more power for that state. Finally, each NPV state would certify its own "national" vote total. But what would happen when news reports suggested election skullduggery somewhere? Would other states really trust, with no power to verify, that state's returns?

The only certain result of NPV would be uncertainty and litigation. In fact, NPV is probably unconstitutional since it ignores the requirement that interstate compacts receive congressional consent. Judges might also believe that the structure of the Constitution's Electoral College clause does imply some outer limit to the power of state legislatures to ignore the will of their own people. It would take a lot of faith in judges, however, to count on them to strike it down. And uncertainty might be part of the objective or at least serve the interests of Electoral College opponents. A similar sand-in-the-gears strategy helped produce the Seventeenth Amendment, which deprived state legislatures of the power to elect U.S. senators.

THE ELECTORAL COLLEGE AND CONSTITUTIONALISM

One danger to all these attacks on the Electoral College is, of course, that we lose the state-by-state system designed by the framers and its protections against regionalism and fraud. This would alter our political ecosystem in some obvious ways – shifting power toward urban centers, for example – but also in ways we cannot predict. Small plurality winners would be more likely; would that lead to a rise of splinter parties and spoiler candidates? Would conservative fears of election fraud in places like Chicago lead to a demand – from the right – for federal control over elections?

The danger, however, is not merely that the attacks succeed in eliminating, or neutering, the Electoral College. The more fundamental risk is that the public adheres to the beliefs that underlie these attacks – that the Constitution is out of date, that the measure of an election is voter self-esteem, and that democracy is an end in itself. All those beliefs can as easily be turned against any of our constitutional checks and balances. The very idea of a constitutional republic is at stake.

The measure of our fundamental law is not whether it actualizes the general will – that was the goal of the French Revolution, not ours. The measure of our Constitution is whether it tends toward justice and those things that support justice, including stability. The Electoral College does this, and we ought not only to preserve it but also to help our fellow Americans understand why it matters.

© 2020 by Trent England

An earlier version of this work appeared in *Imprimis*,
a publication of Hillsdale College.

First American edition published in 2020 by Encounter Books,
an activity of Encounter for Culture and Education, Inc.,
a nonprofit, tax exempt corporation.

Encounter Books website address: www.encounter̶

Manufactured in the United States and pr̶
acid-free paper. The paper used in this publica̶
the minimum requirements of ANSI / NISO z39.48-199̶
(R 1997) (*Permanence of Paper*).

FIRST AMERICAN EDITION

LIBRARY OF CONGRESS CATALOGING-IN-PUBLICATION DATA

Names: England, Trent, author.
Title: Why we must defend the Electoral College / by Trent England.
Description: First American edition. |
New York : Encounter Books, 2020. |
Series: Encounter broadsides; 62 |
Identifiers: LCCN 2020008862 (print) | LCCN 2020008863 (ebook)
| ISBN 9781641771498 (trade paperback) | ISBN 9781641771504 (epub)
Subjects: LCSH: Electoral college—United States. | Presidents—
United States—Election.
Classification: LCC JK529 2020 (print) | LCC JK529 (ebook) |
DDC 324.6/3—dc23
LC record available at https://lccn.loc.gov/2020008862
LC ebook record available at https://lccn.loc.gov/2020008863